# Treatise On Self-Improvement

## Unlock Your Potential

Hichem Karoui

A Global East-West Book

# Table of Contents

# Also by the Author

**Research and Studies**

What is Happiness? An Essay on the Infinite Ways to Find Lasting Joy. "Questions" series. Publisher: Global East-West (London 2023).

Qatar's Options Following Al-Ula Summit: Correct Mistakes or Reproduce the Crisis? (Arabic). Noon publishing in cooperation with the Gulf Future Center ( London – Paris 2021 ). Ebook.

Qatar in Think Tanks and Regional and International Organisations: Qatar in The Eyes of Others Series (2013-2020). Part Three: 2015. (E-Book Published in the USA, June 2021). Arabic.

Qatar in Think Tanks and Regional and International Organisations: Qatar in The Eyes of Others Series (2013-2020) Part Two: 2014. (E-Book Published in the USA, June 2021). Arabic.

Qatar in Think Tanks and Regional and International Organisations: Qatar in The Eyes of Others Series (2013-2020) Part One: 2013. (E-Book Published in the USA, June 2021). Arabic.

The Fifth Column: Islamist objectives in the twenty-first century. Invasion of the West and China. The Gulf Future Center's Papers (London: 2021). Ebook. Arabic.

Revolution, Democracy and Terrorism: Challenges Facing the Arabs. The Gulf Future Center's Papers ( London 2021). E-book. Arabic.

Leadership's Involvement In Institutional

Excellence: Empowerment, Anticipation, Creativity. Noon Publishing (Paris 2020). Ebook. Arabic.

The Apparent Chinese Paradox. Chapter in the collective book "The Syrian Crisis." Springer (2020).

Geopolitical Shifts in the Triangle: The United States, the Gulf Cooperation Council countries, and China. Chapter in the collective book: "Handbook On China and Globalization. " Edward Elgar House (London: 2019), in collaboration with the Center for China and Globalization, Beijing.

Negotiation and Bargaining. Noon Publishing (Paris: 2018). Ebook. Arabic.

Inventing The Middle East. Noon Publishing (Paris: 2018 ). Ebook. Arabic.

U.S. Policy and the Arab-Muslim World: The Understanding Abyss. Noon Publishing (Paris: 2018 ). Ebook. Arabic.

On China And the Arabs. With Dr Gafar Karar Ahmed. Noon Publishing (Paris: 2018 ).

Chatting With My Chinese Friend, KRPC

Publications (Paris: 2016).

Conservative Revolution and Other Essays, KRPC/Middle East Studies, Paris (Paris: 2015 ).

Diplomacy and Conflict: Policy Analyses. Middle-East-Studies/KRPC, (Paris: 2015 ).

Policy Analyses: 2002-2003 (Arabic) Volume 1. KRPC (Paris: 2015).

The Political Algebra of Global Value Change: General Models and Implications for the Muslim World. With Arno Tausch, and Almas Heshmati. Nova Science (New York: 2014).

Middle East Studies in the USA after 9/11(Arabic): Shaping American Perceptions. Nama Centre for Research and Studies (Kingdom of Saudi Arabia: 2013). Arabic.

U.S.- Saudi Love-Hate Story. A Middle East Studies Book. Charleston, S.C. USA. (2013).

Power Revolving Doors: The Shaping of American Perception of Middle East Studies. A Middle East Studies Book. (Charleston, S.C. USA. )

L'administration Bush au Moyen-Orient. (French). Middle East Books ( Paris: 2013).

Arab Spring, The New Middle East in the Making. CS/A Middle East Studies Book. (Charleston, S.C. USA. 2012).

The Bush II Years in the Middle East (2000-2008) A case study in the sociology of international relations. Middle East Books (Paris – South Carolina: 2012).

Diplomacy versus Transparency and Risk Society. Chapter in a collective book: The WikiLeaks Phenomenon: Media and Politics Controversy Between the Virtual and the Real. Arab Center for Research and Policy Studies. (Doha-Beirut: 2012) . Arabic.

Post-Kemalist Politics in Turkey. Chapter in a collective book: The Arabs and Turkey: Present Challenges and Future Bets. The Arab Center for Research and Policy Studies (Doha-Beirut: 2012). Arabic.

Muslims: Nightmare or Strength for Europe? With

Arnaud Tausch. L'Harmattan (Paris: 2011). French.

Where is Saudi Arabia Headed? (French), L'Harmattan (Paris: 2006).

Post – Saddam in Iraq, (French), L'Harmattan (Paris: 2005 ).

The Eagle and the Borders: Prolegomenon to a Critique of the Arab Political Reality. Al-Nawras publishing (Tunisia: 1989). Arabic.

International Balance From Cold War to Détente. Addar Al-Arabiyya (Tunisia: 1985). Arabic.

## Literary Works

Poetry and Mandalas: Colours of Meditation, Global East-West, London, December 2022.

The Invisible Bride: A wise report to a wise minister by a wise citizen (The Morning of the Mogul Book

6), Global East-West, London, January 2023.

Party's Gone? Patria too: A wise report to a wise minister by a wise citizen (The Morning of the Mogul Book 5), Global East-West, London, November 2022.

The Muslim Brothelhood in the Bastille: A wise report to a wise minister by a wise citizen (The Morning of the Mogul Book 4), Global East-West, London, October 2022.

Couvolution and Cooks' Conspiracy: A wise report to a wise minister by a wise citizen (The Morning of the Mogul Book 3), Global East-West, London, October 2022.

James Bond in Jail: A wise report to a wise minister by a wise citizen (The Morning of the Mogul Book 2), Global East-West, London, September 2022.

The Arrival: A wise report to a wise minister by a wise citizen (The Morning of the Mogul Book 1), Global East-West, London, September 2022.

Le secret de Marie.(French Novel) N-Editions. Paris,

2018.

Une affaire d'honneur. (French Novel) N-Editions, Paris, 2018.

4 X 4 : Le tueur frappera quatre fois. (French Novel) N-Editions, Paris 2018.

The Seabook (Arabic Poetry) N-Publishing, Paris, 2018.

Confessions of Blood-Wanted Ahmad (Poetry), KRPC-USA, 2017, (Bilingual: Arabic-English).

Shaman Show (Poetry), KRPC- USA, 2017, (Bilingual: Arabic-English).

Couscous Connexion (French Novel), KRPC, Paris, 2016.

Meurtre au Futuroscope(French Novel), KRPC, Paris, 2016(French).

Seven Pillars of Madness (Arabic Novel), N-Publishing, 2018 (Second Edition). Maison arabe du livre, Tunis, 1983 (First Edition.)

Noon,(Arabic Novel), Demeter, Tunis. (First

edition 1982). N-Publishing (second edition 2016).

# Introduction: How does Self-Improvement Theory work?

*Self-improvement theory is a powerful tool for making positive changes in our lives. It enables us to assess our current situation and identify areas for improvement, such as learning new skills or seeking new experiences. This essay will review the basics of self-improvement theory and how it affects positive change. It will look at the various types of self-improvement goals, strategies for achieving them, and advice on implementing them.*

## *Self-Improvement Theory Definition*

Self-Improvement Theory is an integrative framework that aims to empower people to achieve greater autonomy and self-actualisation through self-directed growth. It is based on the idea that personal development can be attained through a conscious effort by deepening one's understanding of oneself and one's surroundings, cultivating the capacity for reflection and self-regulation, and embracing an openness to learning.

The theory is an interdisciplinary approach to understanding the various psychological and sociocultural factors that influence a person's ability to grow. It investigates how a person's beliefs, motivations, and behaviours are influenced by their environment using a variety of theories, including cognitive-behavioural, psychodynamic, and humanistic perspectives. Finally, this approach seeks to identify ways for individuals to improve their well-being through deliberate effort or intervention.

## *Self-Improvement Theory's Objectives and Benefits*

The Goals and Benefits of the Self-Improvement Theory have been extensively researched and discussed. This theory aims to identify the psychological processes that support successful self-improvement and development. Our understanding of the Goals and Benefits of Self-Improvement Theory has grown significantly in recent years thanks to extensive research conducted by a number of knowledgeable and experienced scholars. Working from a variety of different perspectives, these researchers have greatly informed our understanding of how this theoretical framework can be used to support individual well-being and personal development. In this essay, I'll be discussing some of the most notable contributions made by these scholars, while also exploring the implications that their work has on our understanding of the Goals and Benefits of Self-Improvement Theory. Ultimately, I hope that this essay will serve as a helpful resource to those interested in learning more about this important topic.

According to research, the deliberate use of self-improvement strategies such as goal setting, planning, and problem-solving can increase an individual's self-efficacy and overall well-being. We each have a unique set of genes and characteristics at birth. However, it is through our interactions with others that we grow into fully formed individuals. In order to comprehend how the "self" is socialised, several academics in domains like psychology and sociology have characterised the process of self-development.

# Individual Growth from a Psychological Standpoint

Sigmund Freud (1856-1939) was a prominent psychoanalyst who, in the twentieth century, proposed a hypothesis regarding the origins of individual identity. He identified several phases of development and conjectured that a person's later growth would be contingent on the foundations laid in their youth. A failure to enter or leave a developmental stage appropriately, as proposed by Freud, might have long-lasting psychological and emotional effects.

Erik Erikson (1902-1994) was a psychologist who partly built a theory of personality formation on Freud's ideas. In Erikson's view, however, personality continued to develop and was never complete. His theory consists of eight phases of evolution, beginning with birth and concluding with death. As far as Erikson is concerned, everyone goes through these changes as they mature. Erikson's perspective of self-development, in contrast to Freud's, gave credit to more social components, such as the way we negotiate between our own fundamental wants and what is socially accepted (Erikson, 1982).

Jean Piaget (1896-1980) was a French psychologist who studied the impact of relationships on kids' maturation. The self, he realised, is the product of a dialectic between the internal and external worlds, the mental and the social (Piaget, 1954). We owe a great deal to all three of these philosophers for our current understanding of personal growth.

By monitoring the effects of isolation and maternal deprivation on the development of newborn rhesus monkeys, psychologist Harry Harlow (1905-1981) was able to draw conclusions about the importance of social bonds in human growth. According to Harlow's research, Isolated monkeys display aberrant behaviours like self-harm and have difficulty reintegrating with their social group when reuniting with them. Harlow also experimented with isolating monkeys and exposing them to cloth- and wire-covered surrogate moms. Little monkeys were shown to cling to and take comfort from their cloth moms, suggesting the animals formed attachments to them. After more than seven decades, this study still has implications for psychology, sociology, and development studies.

## Theories of Personal Growth in Sociology

Charles Cooley is often regarded as a forefather of sociological thought (1864–1929). He proposed the concept of "the looking-glass self," which states that individuals' sense of identity is partly formed by their awareness of how others perceive them (Cooley, 1902).

Later, George Herbert Mead (1863-1931) later investigated the concept of the self, an individual's unique identity shaped by societal experiences. To participate in this "self" activity, one must see oneself as others do. That is not something most of us are naturally good at (Mead, 1934). Our ability to empathise with others and see the world from their vantage point is a crucial skill developed via interactions with others. Looking at ourselves through the eyes of the "other" helps us develop empathy and insight into our nature.

When do we transition from helpless infants to fully formed humans with "selves"? There is, according to Mead, a universal sequence of life events through which everyone passes. Children in the formative period can only imitate what they observe, as they cannot conceptualise the world from alternative perspectives. They mimic those with frequent contacts, such as their carers. After this comes to the play phase, in which kids practise acting out different roles. Hence, kids may try on a parent's perspective by mimicking their actions, such as playing house with a toy phone or dressing up as a parent when playing dress-up.

When they play, kids develop the ability to juggle several responsibilities and see how they relate to one another. In addition, they get an appreciation for the complexity of social interactions involving several actors pursuing distinct goals. A youngster of this age, for instance, is probably aware of the many roles that adults play in ensuring a pleasant dining experience in a restaurant (someone will show you to a seat, someone else will take your order, another individual will cook the food, and someone else will wash the dirty dishes).

Ultimately, kids learn about and internalise the generalised other or societal norms for appropriate conduct. At this point in their development, people may picture themselves from other people's perspectives, allowing them to establish a sense of "self" from a sociological point of view (Mead, 1934; Mead, 1964).

## *Towards a Theory of Moral Development: Kohlberg's*

The process of socialisation includes the cultivation of moral principles. Learning what constitutes "good" and "bad" in a particular culture is crucial to the well-being of any civilisation. Those who have matured morally are able to control their impulses and think more about the more significant benefit of society and their fellow humans. The development of moral judgement was an area of study for Lawrence Kohlberg (1927-1987). He did this by proposing a three-stage theory of moral evolution, which he called "pre-conventional," "conventional," and "post-conventional," to explain how people go from one stage to the next.

Children at the pre-conventional stage rely only on their senses to understand the environment since they have not yet developed the higher-level cognitive abilities necessary to understand it. The traditional idea emerges throughout the adolescent years when children grow more sensitive to the emotions of others and begin to factor those emotions into their evaluations of "good" and "bad." At the last post-conventional stage, individuals begin to conceive of morality in more universal, abstract terms, such as the notion that every person should have the right to be guaranteed the pursuit of happiness, life, and liberty. In addition, at this point, most people are aware that legality and morality are not necessarily on equal footing (Kohlberg, 1981). Hundreds of thousands of Tunisians and Egyptians used post-conventional morality when they took to the streets in 2011 to protest government corruption. They realised that despite their government's legitimacy, it was immoral.

## *The Role of Gender in Gilligan's Theory of Moral Growth*

As Kohlberg's study was done primarily on male individuals, another sociologist, Carol Gilligan (1936-), noticed that his theory might indicate gender bias. Might we expect a different reaction from female participants? Would a female social scientist see different trends while evaluating the data? She set out to investigate whether there were gender-specific variations in the moral development of young boys and girls. Gilligan found evidence to support the idea that males and females view morality differently. Young men looked to have a justice-oriented worldview that puts a premium on following the rules. On the other hand, girls appear to have a worldview characterised by concern and responsibility; they are more likely to try to understand the motivations behind actions that may initially appear immoral.

Gilligan is accurate that it would have been ideal if Kohlberg's study had included both sexes. However, the lack of diversity in the sample has led to the study's scientific discrediting. Similarly, no one has been able to reproduce Gilligan's findings from this study. Gilligan concluded that the inequalities he saw in morality did not stem from a lack of moral development but rather from inadequate socialisation. Gender socialisation, the practice of instructing young boys and girls in the cultural norms and behaviours expected of them depending on their sex (see "What a Beautiful Little Lady"), is responsible for the observed differences in male and female conduct.

Gilligan acknowledged that Kohlberg's approach assumed the justice perspective to be correct or superior. On the other hand, Gilligan argued that the two standards of justice were complementary rather than competing. The bottom line, she said, is that ladies are taught to be nurturing and caring at home, while boys are taught to be rule-followers in the workplace (Gilligan, 1982; Gilligan, 1990).

## An Overview of Various Techniques

The Self-Improvement Theory Goals and Benefits are multifaceted and extensive. At its core, this theory aims to increase individuals' autonomy by empowering them to take control of their own lives. Individuals can develop an understanding of their strengths and weaknesses, and a heightened sense of responsibility for their learning and development, by focusing on self-awareness and personal growth.

Self-improvement theory is a relatively new field of study investigating how people can improve their lives. It entails delving into various topics such as self-efficacy, goal setting, and cognitive restructuring. Self-improvement theory techniques such as mindfulness meditation, positive visualisation, and behaviour modification provide a variety of development strategies. This theory is a field of study that looks into how people can improve their well-being, satisfaction, and sense of self-worth. It has grown in popularity in recent years to provide insight into how individuals can improve their psychological functioning. Cognitive restructuring, positive reinforcement, goal setting, problem-solving, and mindfulness meditation are examples of self-improvement theory techniques.

### Developing a Positive Attitude

Adopting a Positive Mindset is a concept that entails the deliberate cultivation of a positive outlook on life. It includes a resilient, growing, and self-efficacy attitude that can be developed through intentional cognitive and behavioural strategies. Individuals can cultivate an optimistic mindset by prioritising positive thoughts over negative ones and engaging in activities that promote well-being. This leads to improved psychological functioning.

Adopting a Positive Mindset is a way of life that

seeks to embrace and cultivate an optimistic mental attitude. It is based on the idea that the quality of one's thoughts has a direct and causal impact on one's behaviour, feelings, and overall well-being.

## Self-Awareness Training

The process of actively engaging in reflective thought and reflection about one's thoughts, feelings, and behaviours is called practising self-awareness. It is a cognitive skill that entails awareness of one's internal state, including mental health, biases, values, strengths, and weaknesses. As a result, practising self-awareness can assist individuals in gaining greater insight into their behaviour and thus making more informed life decisions. It can be defined as a person's deliberate effort to observe and comprehend their own cognitive, emotional, and behavioural states. This entails continuously inquiring into one's thoughts, feelings, behaviours, and motivations to understand oneself better.

## *Making Changes and Taking Action*

Taking action and changing one's environment is a process of actively engaging with one's environment in order to modify it to suit one's goals better. It entails assessing the current situation, developing solutions, and implementing them. Individuals must be willing to accept personal responsibility for their actions and the consequences of those decisions. Furthermore, taking action necessitates a willingness to learn from mistakes and adjust strategies as needed. Taking action and making changes is a personal transformation process that involves an individual critically examining their perspectives, values, and habits and then taking deliberate steps to change them. It necessitates developing awareness of one's current situation and a willingness to challenge long-held beliefs or approaches that may impede the individual's growth. One example is adopting new strategies in communication, learning, problem-solving, decision-making, and other areas of life where change is desired.

## The Advantages of Applying Theory

The application of self-improvement theory is expected to yield various benefits by allowing individuals to pursue a more comprehensive approach to personal development. This can be accomplished through increased self-awareness and a greater understanding of how one's behaviour and attitude affect how one interacts with others. Furthermore, this theoretical framework can provide direction for those unsure or unmotivated in their current circumstances and tools to make meaningful changes. Self-improvement theory has the potential to offer several tangible benefits. It can, for example, promote higher levels of emotional intelligence and resilience, allowing people to manage their emotions and stressors better. It can also increase have an innate ability to adapt and adjust their behaviours, attitudes, and outlooks to manage hostile conditions better. According to self-improvement theory, individuals can effectively navigate difficult circumstances by learning from past experiences, developing insight into one's strengths and weaknesses, and actively engaging in meaningful activities.

- **Unfavourable working conditions**

Competition is unavoidable, but we should make it a positive type that helps us improve our skills and talents. Negativity and overachievement can harm relationships and mental health, so practise self-care and watch for those around you!

Dog-eat-dog thinking, in which everyone is looking for an advantage, should be avoided at all costs. It's an ideal environment for a cynic to thrive. No one will appreciate your efforts even if you skip meals and work late. There is sometimes too much work to do, and no one cares enough to pitch in and help. Keep your distance. It is not appropriate for your pride. There are competition stakes everywhere. Maintain a level of fitness that allows you to compete, but only on an equal playing field.

- **Other people's actions**

Bulldozers, brown-nosers, snitches, whiners, backstabbers, snipers, the walking wounded, controllers, nags, complainers, bomb-throwers, and patronisers should all be avoided. These people will undermine your self-esteem and derail your efforts to improve yourself.

- **Change Must Be Accepted**

Being a green beetle in a brown grassland is

impossible. The winds of change put our worldviews to the test. It forces us to think outside the box and tests our adaptability. Life may become more difficult as we adjust to these changes, and we may experience some anxiety. However, because constant change is unavoidable, we must learn to adapt.

### • Previous Work Experience

It is acceptable to cry and exclaim "ouch!" in pain. But don't let your despair turn into terror. It could catch your tail and swing you around. Instead, each setback and error should be viewed as a learning opportunity.

### • Negative Worldview

Look at what you're looking at. Avoid being surrounded by the world's negativity. Instead, we must learn how to make the best of bad situations to boost our self-esteem.

- **Determinism**

Individuals' personalities and character traits are a product of their genetic makeup, psychological development, and social and physical environments, which include their families, workplaces, and social networks. You are a one-of-a-kind individual in your own right. Just because your father made a mistake doesn't mean you will, too. Learn from the mistakes of others so that you don't make the same ones.

# 1 – What is the Purpose of Self-Improvement?

*This chapter will examine the relationship between success and personal development and how we can use it to our advantage.*

In our increasingly fast-paced world, every minute must be filled with meaningful activities and accomplishments. Self-improvement is essential to modern life, from improving our diets to picking up a new hobby. But why are we so obsessed with self-improvement? Is the end goal solely financial? Or is there more to the idea of living a fulfilled life? To answer these questions, let's define "self-improvement" and how it can affect our finances, both positively and negatively.

### *Introduction to Self-Improvement: What is the Goal?*

Self-improvement aims to strive to be the best version of ourselves. It entails identifying areas for improvement and then taking actionable steps to make changes and achieve our objectives. Personal relationships, career development, health and fitness, creativity, and other areas of life can all benefit from self-improvement. It is about setting attainable goals for ourselves, learning how to stay motivated over time, and honing the skills required to achieve our goals. Self-improvement has numerous advantages. It can result in increased self-esteem and confidence, better mental clarity and focus, better physical health, increased productivity in daily tasks and activities, and tremendous success in personal and professional endeavours. We can gain insight into our strengths and weaknesses while cultivating new habits to help us achieve our goals through self-improvement. It also helps us become more aware of our thoughts and actions, allowing us to have a healthier relationship with ourselves and the world around us.

### *What does it mean to be self-improved?*

Self-improvement is the process of consciously making changes to become the best possible version of oneself. It necessitates introspection and an understanding of what needs to be improved, followed by an active pursuit of knowledge, experience, and personal development through activities such as learning new skills, setting goals, and developing healthy habits. Self-improvement can apply to any aspect of a person's life, including the body, mind, relationships, and career. It is frequently used to describe a desire to improve oneself physically, mentally, emotionally, or spiritually.

Health and wellness initiatives such as working out more regularly or improving nutrition are standard components, as are educational enrichment activities such as taking classes or reading; personal growth activities such as journaling or meditating; career advancement through workshops and seminars; and relationship improvement through communication exercises or public speaking practise. Self-improvement encompasses all aspects of life that can make a person better in some way, such as developing core values, deepening relationships with others, and pursuing meaningful achievements.

### *How people use self-improvement in their daily lives*

Self-improvement is a powerful tool for bringing about positive change in our lives. It can assist us in learning new skills, gaining confidence, and setting goals. It is an ongoing self-development journey that necessitates dedication and commitment. Anyone, with proper planning, can use self-improvement techniques to improve their capabilities and achieve their desired goals. Understanding your strengths and weaknesses and identifying areas for improvement is the first step towards self-improvement. You can identify areas that require focus and effort by honestly assessing yourself. Once you gain clarity about what needs to be done, you can create a plan for action which will give you the necessary tools to reach your goals.

Setting achievable goals, learning new skills, developing new habits, or making lifestyle changes such as diet or exercise regimes are all part of this. Self-improvement includes mental development as well as physical changes, such as accepting criticism positively, having a positive attitude, or ameliorating communication skills. You should work on developing a better understanding of yourself and others around you, as well as building relationships with people who will help you achieve your personal goals.

### *Why do people strive to better themselves?*

People strive to be better for a variety of reasons. Self-improvement can refer to anything from changing bad habits to improving one's mental health to working on one's personal skills and talents. For many, it is an ongoing journey that entails setting goals and stepping outside of one's comfort zone. *In some cases, a traumatic event, as well as feelings of unhappiness or dissatisfaction with life in general, may motivate self-improvement.* People frequently recognise that in order to reach their full potential, they must work on personal development. This could include learning a new skill or taking steps to improve relationships with others. People may also seek self-improvement in order to be more successful at work or to boost their overall self-confidence. Striving for improvement, for whatever reason, is a joint endeavour shared by many people from all walks of life.

## Personal development is critical to your success.

Everything that occurs to us serves a purpose. There are times when one event can set off another. Instead of isolating yourself out of fear and wallowing in self-loathing over past hurts, embarrassments, and failures, view them as valuable life lessons and apply them to become a better, stronger, and more successful version of yourself.

Success and personal development are two interconnected components. To succeed in life, one must strive for continuous growth and improvement. Personal development is an ongoing process that necessitates self-reflection, motivation, and commitment. Everyone's road to success is unique, but the emphasis should always be on self-improvement and striving for greatness.

To be successful in life, one must prioritise self-development and growth. It is necessary to make an ongoing effort to improve one's personal qualities and skill sets. Proactivity and commitment are essential when striving for development and improvement; with these two components, progress is likely to continue.

A continuous commitment to self-evaluation, reflection, and learning is required to identify areas for improvement and capitalise on them through conscious decision-making. By committing to this constant growth and metamorphosis process, one can maximise opportunities while also developing into a more resilient, adaptive, and dynamic individual.

Did you watch Patch Adams' movie? It's an excellent film that will motivate you to be a better person. Hunter Adams, also known as "patch," is a medical student who failed the licensure exams. After months of sadness, despair, and suicide attempts, he sought medical attention and voluntarily checked himself into a mental institution. He interacted with many patients during his months in the hospital—individuals who are unhealthy in that regard. One of them was catatonic. Another was mentally challenged. Another example was schizophrenia. Patch learned self-restoration techniques and realised he needed to start over and get his life back on track. He awoke one morning with the realisation that, despite his many setbacks and difficulties, he still wanted to pursue a career in medicine. His positive attitude has resulted in personal growth and achievement. He improved not only his own life but also the lives of those around him. What kind of an impact did he have? He excelled in medicine and rose to become one of the best doctors in his country.

Two questions arise:

*First, when does working on one's own improvement become a requirement for success?*

The concept of 'betterment' is intriguing because it assumes that personal development and improvement are necessary prerequisites for success. It is critical to recognise that the journey towards self-improvement is essential in order to achieve anything. Working on yourself has thus become crucial for success. In this way, the modern world has evolved into a place where self-improvement is essential for advancement. With its emphasis on achievement and success, today's world has created a culture in which people are constantly striving to better themselves. This concept of constantly improving has become an essential part of modern life and has helped many ordinary people succeed. Modern society has also evolved, making it nearly impossible to achieve anything without working on one's own improvement.

*Second, where do we even start?*

Self-improvement is a multifaceted endeavour that requires an individual  to assess their current state and make a conscious decision to strive for improvement. This also necessitates putting in place a structured plan that makes use of available resources and strategies to achieve the desired results. To foster growth, one must also understand one's psychological, emotional, and behavioural aspects. Before you can improve yourself, you must first consider your values, beliefs, and goals. It is critical to look for any underlying psychological issues influencing a person's behaviour and to consider how they interact with their surroundings. Once this is completed, it will be simple to identify problem areas and devise solutions to them. As the individual progresses through different stages of life, the process of self-improvement should be ongoing. As they grow and mature, their values, beliefs, and motivations will shift. As a result, it is critical to assess one's progress towards self-improvement on a regular basis.

## *To summarise, follow this advice:*

- Stop treating yourself as a failure, both mentally and physically. It would help if you first accept yourself in order to be accepted by others.

- Rather than wallow in self-pity, consider how to emulate the studs and supermodels you see on TV. You need more than great legs or a six-pack to boost your confidence. Instead, focus on your inner beauty.

- When people ask for your help, please encourage them to look beyond their low self-esteem. Avoid lowering yourself to their level. They will drag you down with them until you feel unhappy and worthless.

- There is more space for you to grow from your accomplishments than your mistakes. Simply because you received a low score on a scientific test does not mean you are a complete moron doomed to live the rest of your life in misery. There will always be a second chance. So make room for growth in your life.

- Avoid taking too much at once. You can't expect a black sheep to behave just by waving your hand. Making progress towards self-improvement necessitates perseverance and a willingness to take things day by day.

- Personal development leads to psychological stability, growth, and success. It is the result of feeling good about oneself and having a healthy regard for one's own worth.

- Create goals that are important to you and that you can achieve. If you want to look like Cameron Diaz or Ralph Fiennes, you'll need more than just self-improvement. The goal is for YOU to become stronger and better.

- Some people place a high value on seemingly insignificant details. A simple pat on the back, a friendly "hi" or "hello," a hearty "good day," or a remark like "hey, I love your tie!" can make Mr Smith's day. People find us more appealing when we take the time to notice and appreciate the beauty all around us, including in other people.

- Just because you're willing to change your habits and improve yourself doesn't mean everyone else is. We live in a society where people of widely disparate morals and perspectives coexist. If you and your closest friend appear to share many interests, she may be unwilling to join you on a quest for personal development.

- We must always keep in mind that "overnight success" does not exist. It's always a wonderful feeling to cling to what you already have, knowing that it was once just one of the things you wished for. "When the learner is ready, the instructor will appear," a lovely quote says. We've all come to learn something new. It is critical to remember that "overnight success" is a myth in order to stay grounded and focused on our goals. It can also be satisfying to hold on to our accomplishments while remembering that they were once nothing more than dreams. The proverb reminds us that with dedication and hard work, we can achieve our goals. Our teachers include our parents, school teachers, friends, coworkers, officemates, and neighbours. When we are open to self-improvement, we increase our chances of success.

# Capital and Social Capital

*"The goal of self-improvement is to take deliberate action and positive strides towards one's full potential. It entails self-reflection, goal setting, and purposeful action to achieve real progress towards better success, happiness, and wellness."*

If you're anything like the rest of us, making more money is probably something that has crossed your mind. But suppose we took a new approach? Is material success the end goal of striving for excellence, or do we have higher aspirations? To answer this question, I will look at the motivations of those who seek self-improvement and the consequences of a narrow focus on financial gain. We may find a more profound and significant explanation for self-improvement if we look beneath our ambition for advancement.

## *The Importance of Money in Personal Development*

While it is unnecessary, financial support can be helpful during personal development. For example, you could use it to enrol in a course, visit new places and experience new cultures, or buy books and other resources that expand your knowledge. To concentrate on what is truly important in life—your development and growth—money makes such endeavours more feasible and less of a financial burden. Without money, however, self-improvement is still attainable.

Learning doesn't have to cost a thing, thanks to the wealth of freely accessible materials both online and in physical libraries. Mentors, friends, and family members are additional resources to tap for assistance. Reading an inspirational book or joining a support group are two growth-promoting pursuits that only cost time or energy. As a bonus, many organisations offer financial aid to students who show academic promise but need more means to continue their education beyond high school. Although it's not required, money does help those who are working to better themselves. If you lack the means to invest in your personal development, that doesn't mean you can't still do so; it just means you'll have to find other ways to get there insofar as your dedication continues to be unwavering. An exceptional writer must sit down and crank out a 5,000-word article. Before diving in headfirst, it's essential to commit to the project at hand and maintain that dedication so to create something truly remarkable. A lack of determination and drive can undermine the results of the entire article-writing process. Doing so requires giving the project one's full attention, conducting extensive research, and becoming thoroughly versed in one's chosen topic so that one may write about it with credibility and expertise. Create a riveting piece of writing by learning to hold the reader's attention and interest through suspense and other techniques. Remember the importance of being clear and concise when writing on an assignment. After you've laid out the article's major points, it's time to fill them out with more detail and flair. To accomplish this, you should use straightforward language and specific examples to paint a clear picture of the scene and the mood you want to convey.

Try to utilise exciting plot twists and suspenseful elements to keep readers engaged throughout and ensure that all facts and details are accurate and up-to-date.

Lastly, write from your heart and be true to your unique voice as you work to create an article that you can be proud of.

### *Money as a motivator for self-improvement*

Do you ever wonder why so many people strive to be better versions of themselves? It's tempting to fall back on the concept that it's all about enhancing our quality of life or simply becoming a more excellent version of ourselves. But could money be the secret motivator behind most self-improvement efforts? Is making more money the primary goal of self-improvement? To answer these questions, I'll delve deep into why people seek to improve themselves and whether it's about growing their money accounts.

Money may be a powerful incentive for self-improvement in both the professional and personal worlds. On the professional front, you can spend money to fund training or education that will help you enhance your career. Investing in yourself with money or time will set you up for long-term success. Furthermore, if you have particular financial goals that need you to save more, such as building an emergency fund or paying off debt, having a precise amount to accomplish is typically enough motivation to boost earnings and reduce expenditure. Money can provide incentives to improve yourself and become a better version of yourself personally. You may discover that financially challenging yourself drives you to adopt healthier lifestyle choices, such as exercising consistently or eating healthy meals. Furthermore, when working on long-term financial goals, such as travel plans or house improvements, having a deadline to meet these goals pushes us even more. When we compare our current financial status to our desired financial future state, we are often motivated to put in the effort required for progress. Ultimately, money should not impede self-improvement motivation.

***The potential advantages of having more money in pursuing self-improvement.***

Money is commonly regarded as the most powerful motivation for self-improvement. But does this spark of ambition necessarily have to be for a bigger paycheck? Is money still the ultimate aim for personal growth and development in an age when fulfilment and meaning are sought more? To address this question, we must first understand the origins of modern self-improvement—what motivates people to strive for something bigger than themselves? We can then decide whether money gain should be the sole goal of our development activities.

One potential advantage of having more money in pursuing self-improvement is that it can enable access to resources and opportunities that would otherwise be unavailable. Those with financial security may be able to get professional help for difficulties such as mental health, pursue personal development activities such as coaching or mentorship, and acquire access to luxury things that can make life easier or more joyful.

Furthermore, having extra money allows you to pursue your dreams and job goals more freely. Those with greater financial security have more options for extending their education, obtaining higher-paying employment, and exploring alternative kinds of revenue generating.

Finally, financial freedom can provide opportunities for travel, leisure activities, and even philanthropy, providing greater satisfaction and personal growth. More money for self-improvement allows access to resources and opportunities that might otherwise be unavailable. Still, it can also lead to higher overall satisfaction, which implies acquiring luxury products that make life easier or even more fun. It also provides a degree of independence that allows individuals to explore other alternatives and widen their horizons while aiming for self-improvement.

### *The dangers of making money the primary goal of self-improvement.*

Many people believe that self-improvement is only about making more money. But, unfortunately, we live in a culture where riches and collecting more items define success, so it's tempting to believe that spending our time trying to better ourselves will lead to increased earning potential and more expensive lifestyles.

Nonetheless, pursuing self-improvement should be centred on human progress rather than monetary rewards. When money is the primary goal of self-improvement, it is easy to ignore other crucial areas of life. Instead of gaining new skills, creating stronger relationships, and practising self-care, people may devote their time and energy to discovering new methods to make money. While money is a crucial aspect of constructing a solid and secure future, *focusing entirely on money can lead to feelings of discontent or mild depression and a lack of balance between work and leisure activities,* which can influence physical and mental health. Furthermore, *when people devote all their work to earning money, they may fail to see their personal value or worth beyond what they have materially.* This can lead to a lowered feeling of self-worth and a tendency to judge others only on their financial prosperity. When people concentrate significantly on making money, they may overlook other vital parts of life. It's easy to get *mired in a loop of always trying for financial gain,* leaving no time or energy for learning, establishing relationships, or caring for oneself.

*This cycle may result in increased stress, worry, and physical illnesses owing to a lack of balance between work and leisure activities.* Furthermore, continuing to follow this pattern might lead to an inability to realise the importance of one's value beyond money or worth outside of their income. This may eventually result in people feeling alone and inadequate or being critical of others based purely on their financial advantages.

Never forget: Self-improvement is a continuous process that assists us in identifying and overcoming obstacles to achieve our goals. It entails constantly upgrading our expectations, pushing ourselves to step beyond our comfort zone, and striving for greatness in all facets of life.

Stop considering yourself a second-rate human being. Forget the never-ending circle of "If only I were wealthy... if only I were tiny," and so on. The first step towards self-improvement is embracing yourself as you are. Next, we must stop comparing ourselves to others to discover that we have ten more reasons to envy them.

Everyone has insecurities. Nobody is faultless. We constantly desire more extraordinary items, qualities, physiological parts, and so forth. But life does not have to be perfect for people to be happy with themselves.

Self-improvement and self-love do not entail proclaiming to the world that you are lovely and the best. Instead, it is the virtue of contentment and acceptance; we begin to feel comfortable and cheerful when we start to better ourselves.

## Connections, Self-Improvement and Money

When it comes to making more money, sure people want the following benefits: They develop more relationships.

As a general rule, the more money you have, the

higher your sense of self-worth. Basically, if you have a positive outlook on life and yourself, you'll be able to earn and keep more money. But while producing more money, confident people enjoy the following advantages: They build more connections. *There is a link between self-esteem, capital, and social capital.*

Self-improvement is essential to living a whole and successful life, regardless of employment, status, or lifestyle. Money is a crucial aspect of self-improvement. Money significantly impacts your potential to develop yourself and your life. Money can be used to acquire educational materials, improve health and wellness, or provide access to resources that help you develop your talents in areas such as leadership. Appropriate investment in these areas will give you an advantage in growing yourself and creating significant changes in your life. Financial independence also provides more outstanding options for leisure interests, like travel, which can enhance your perspective on the world. Not only does having enough money offer more resources to help you make these adjustments, but it also provides a sense of stability from any financial worries or anxieties. Those who are financially secure are able to focus more on the goals they have set for themselves without the added burden of worrying about bills or expenses. Furthermore, having access to finances allows you more leeway in taking chances with various investments that could contribute to personal progress. It provides a cushion so that if something does not go as planned, the consequences are less severe than in other cases. Money allows people to pursue their passions and aspirations while decreasing the overall stress of managing finances.

## Financial incentives for personal development

You may often find yourself pondering the motivation behind people's efforts to improve themselves. It's tempting to think that happiness and contentment are the ultimate goals. But may financial gain be the hidden impetus for most attempts at self-improvement? Is monetary gain the primary goal of self-improvement? Is its end goal a more significant bank balance?

Gaining financial stability can be a powerful incentive for personal and professional development. Regarding your work, money might help you pay for classes or certifications that will move you up the ranks. In addition, spending time or money on improving yourself will pay dividends in the long run. More importantly, having a substantial amount to target is typically enough motivation to raise wages and restrict spending if you have clear financial goals that need you to save more, like establishing an emergency fund or paying off debt. When it comes to bettering oneself, financial rewards might serve as motivation. Self-financing goals can be an excellent way to motivate yourself to adopt better habits like regular exercise and nutritious food planning. Furthermore, having a deadline linked with reaching these goals typically pushes us to work harder towards them. This is especially true when saving for long-term goals like vacations or home improvements.

When we compare our current financial status to our anticipated financial future state, we are frequently motivated to put in the effort required for progress. Many believe financial gain is the most crucial personal development and growth incentive. But should the driving force behind one's aim always be a financial success? Is financial success still the be-all and end-all of life improvement in an era where meaning and fulfilment are prized above all else?

Having additional financial resources may help one better themselves since it may make previously inaccessible tools and opportunities available. Those who are financially stable are in a better position to address pressing needs like mental health care, engage in enriching experiences like coaching or mentoring and purchase convenience and pleasure goods that make their lives better or more pleasurable. And the financial independence that comes from earning more can be used to pursue personal and professional aspirations. If one's financial situation improves, they are in a better position to pursue opportunities for professional development, higher salary, and diversified sources of revenue. Last but not least, the flexibility afforded by financial independence can lead to increased personal growth and contentment through experiences such as travel, leisure pursuits, and even charitable giving. One's level of contentment might rise due to having more disposable income to invest in personal development. This allows for pursuing goals that might otherwise be out of reach.

***Financial assistance may enable people to advance in their professional and academic careers.***

With more money, you may invest in personal development options such as coaching and mentoring programmes, mental health counselling, physically active hobbies, and charity giving. Additionally, a higher income enables the purchase of lavish luxuries that can improve one's quality of life. Financial stability opens the door to independence, essential for developing one's potential and realising one's dreams.

Remember: Continuous attempts to develop oneself allow us to notice and overcome the obstacles that stand in the way of our goals. Optimism requires us to remain in a perpetual state of progress, pushing ourselves to break out of our routines and settle for nothing less than the best in whatever we do.

Please cease thinking of yourself as anything less than a whole human being. Stop the endless cycle of "If only I were rich... If only I were little," and so on. Accepting oneself is the first step towards self-improvement. The next stage is to stop comparing ourselves to others and find ten more things to envy.

To some extent, this is correct. Nobody is perfect. We are continually looking for better traits, features, organs, etc. However, people can be happy even if their lives aren't perfect.

Attempting to persuade the world that you are the

most beautiful and finest person is not an act of self-improvement or self-love. Instead, self-esteem is boosted, and progress towards happiness is aided by cultivating qualities like contentment and acceptance.

Self-improvement aims to develop one's abilities to their fullest potential through conscious effort and progress. Reflection, goal-setting, and proactive action may improve achievement, happiness, and well-being.

## The Financial Effect of Personal Growth

In general, the more money you have, the better your feeling of self-worth. Fundamentally, if you have a good attitude about life and yourself, you can make and keep more money.

The following things favour financially secure people: They are better networkers. Financial success is associated with higher levels of self-esteem.

Fundamentally, if you have a good attitude about life and yourself, you can make and keep more money. In short, they are better networkers.

Regardless of your background, self-improvement is necessary for a happy and successful life. When considering methods to better oneself, financial issues are always an issue. Your financial means heavily impact the amount of room you have for personal and professional development. Financial security helps you to invest in your future by paying for your education, boosting your health, and expanding your leadership potential. Spending time and energy on these areas of personal development can put you in a better position to make positive life changes.

Increased time and finances for hobbies and interests such as travel may assist in broadening one's perspectives when financial security is reached. Not only may financial stability give additional resources to help with these improvements, but it can also provide emotional peace of mind. People who don't have to worry about making ends meet can concentrate on attaining their ambitions.

Additionally, if you have money, you can experiment with different investments to help you grow individually. It gives some wiggle room if things don't go as planned, limiting the harm that may otherwise ensue. Finally, financial security helps people focus on what matters to them while alleviating the budgeting pressure.

# 2 – A Crucial Role in Your Success

*It is no secret that success takes hard work and dedication, but the path to success can be made much easier with self-improvement. Self-improvement is vital to success, allowing you to become the best version of yourself. If you work on yourself, you can give yourself the knowledge and skills to reach your goals and objectives. Self-improvement also helps boost confidence and improve motivation to focus on achieving success.*

Wishing "I was someone else" is a common reaction

when we feel trapped by self-doubt, anxiety, and insecurity. Most of the time, we assume that everyone else is better than us, while most people are just timider than us. The need to improve yourself is the first step towards succeeding in life. If you want to become better, then start by identifying your strengths and weaknesses, as well as your areas for improvement.

## Alpha and Beta

For example, you are at a party when you see a stunning woman sitting alone and enjoying a drink. It occurs to you that she exudes an air of serene assurance. Thought clouds would form in her see-through brain, and you could be surprised to learn that she wonders, "are people talking about why I have sat here alone? Why don't boys find me attractive? My ankles are too small for my taste. I wish I was as smart as my best buddy." Her facial expressions tell you that she appears very insecure and unhappy. This is the typical Beta girl.

If you were to talk to her, she would be surprised and flattered. She has no idea how attractive she is to men. Yet, her mind is not clouded with insecurities and doubt.

The "Alpha Girl" is just the opposite type of character. These girls are simple to identify. They are the ones surrounded by boys and men. They have an invisible force field that repels women and attracts men. They usually have an air of superiority about them. Their smiles are genuine, not forced. They appear to be the most confident, but not in a cocky way. They are very friendly but not fake or phoney.

When we see a young person at the helm of a successful firm, our first thought is, "Wooh...." What more could he possibly want?  But we don't know that he examines his reflection in the mirror while muttering, "I loathe my large eyes. How come nobody wants to hang out with me? Please, I wish my parents could still get along." Just think about it. Doesn't it make you laugh? Everyone has at least one person in their life who they secretly wish they could switch places with because of how ridiculously wonderful they seem. As a result, we tend to feel uneasy around others who share our insecurities. Our silent desperation causes us to have poor self-worth, little self-confidence, and no will to better ourselves. It is impossible to change who we are, but we can change our perspective.

### *How to change?*

The first step to understanding ourselves is to realise that we are not the only ones uncomfortable in social situations. It's uncommon to be the last person to realise that you have an annoying habit like chewing your fingernails or having a filthy tongue. We must first understand that we have weaknesses and faults, which don't make us bad people. We can learn to appreciate our flaws for what they are, as well as the strengths that lie within them. It's easier than you think.

I know a person who is a talker. She can babble for hours. As a result, she is usually the only one in a discussion whose opinion is expected. So, people we know in common don't hang out with each other when she's around, and she has no idea how much of an impact she has on those around her. As a result, she feels ignored and misunderstood. To help her, one needs to remind her that talking incessantly is not necessarily the greatest gift in the world. There is no better way to improve yourself than by talking to and listening to a reliable buddy. You should seek out a person with whom you feel safe discussing anything, even delicate matters. Pose queries such as, "Do I usually sound so argumentative?" or "Does my breath smell?" or "Do you think I am ill-mannered?" or "Do you think I am pretty?" or "Am I annoying you right now?"  In this approach, it will be apparent to the other person that you value personal development. Listen when the other has something to say, even if you want to tell them, "don't exaggerate!"  Keep an open mind and heart.

## *Self-Love*

The best love of all is learning to love oneself. A lot of this is correct! Self-love is a prerequisite for a genuine love of others. Remember that it is impossible to give away something you do not own.

Self-love is an essential factor in building strong relationships with others. Humans often seek love from their family, friends, and significant others. But for real love to be shared, it must start within ourselves first. We must learn and use habits that make us better people if we want to know who we are and love ourselves no matter what.

Showing love requires time and effort; it's a process that doesn't happen overnight. It means getting to know our strengths and weaknesses to work on them better. Additionally, part of loving ourselves means caring for ourselves - physically, mentally, emotionally, and spiritually. When these aspects are taken care of, we become more content with who we are as individuals, which makes it easier to extend true love outwardly towards those around us too!

Put yourself out there as a living, breathing example of the benefits of self-improvement before you try to lecture anybody else on the subject. To become better people, we must first work to better ourselves; only then can we hope to inspire others to do the same, and ultimately the rest of the world.

Good relationships are built on trust and open communication. When you feel comfortable with a friend, you can be yourself, with all your flaws.

## Self-Esteem

Developing a healthy sense of self-worth is difficult, but it is crucial to leading a happy life. Self-esteem is our opinion of ourselves, affecting our behaviour and interactions with others. First, however, we must understand that our self-esteem is not set in stone but something that can be changed and improved.

The first step to building self-esteem is to *recognise your negative thoughts and beliefs about yourself.* Once these are identified, it is important to challenge them and replace them with more positive ones. This can be done by writing down the negative thoughts and then writing down a more positive thought or affirmation to replace them.

Another way to build self-esteem is to *focus on your strengths and accomplishments.* Take time to recognise your successes, no matter how small. Celebrate your victories, and remember to give yourself credit when you do something well.

It is also important to practice self-care. Improving your sense of self is as simple as prioritising your health on all fronts. This could include getting enough sleep, eating healthy foods, exercising regularly, engaging in activities that make you happy, and spending time with people who make you feel good about yourself.

Finally, it is essential to remember that building self-esteem takes time and effort. It will take time, but you will eventually see results if you stay consistent with your efforts.

## *What is self-esteem, and why is it so important?*

*Self-Esteem* can be defined as an individual's subjective evaluation of their worth. It is a cognitive construct that reflects the appraisal of one's positive or negative self-concept based on perceived successes and failures in various domains of life. Self-esteem is believed to be underpinned by multiple psychological mechanisms, such as attributions, feedback loops, and affective responses, as well as social comparison processes. It has been theorised as a multi-dimensional construct of global self-worth, perceived competence, and perceived attractiveness. Self-esteem can be positive or negative, influencing a person's behaviours, emotions, and relationships.

Self-esteem is how we think, feel, and act about ourselves. It is essential to our overall mental health as it helps us understand who we are, how we fit in, and how we meet life's challenges. It impacts our relationships and our ability to cope when things do not go our way, and it determines the amount of respect we have for ourselves. Self-esteem can be high, low, or somewhere in between. It changes over time and fluctuates depending on our circumstances. A positive self-image entails not having an unrealistically high or debilitating opinion of oneself. It helps you see your strengths and weaknesses objectively. It allows you to take risks and stand up for yourself when necessary. People with healthy self-esteem tend to be more confident, resilient, and better equipped to handle criticism than those with lower self-esteem, who lack confidence and struggle with decision-making. Low self-esteem can also lead to depression, anxiety, or loneliness as individuals become increasingly hard on themselves or compare themselves negatively to others. Building a solid sense of self-worth is essential to maturing and managing life.

Self-esteem is closely related to self-concept, the individual's perception of themselves. It is formed from a combination of beliefs, experiences, and evaluations that an individual has about their abilities, role in society, and sense of worth. Self-esteem has several positive psychological functions; it serves as an internal motivator, enhances our capacity for dealing with stress, influences our performance and behaviour in social situations, and helps us establish relationships with others. Individuals with high self-esteem have higher levels of emotional well-being than those with lower levels of self-esteem, who are more prone to emotional distress. Studies have found that increasing one's self-esteem can bring about positive changes in an individual's physical health since people tend to take better care of themselves when they have tremendous respect for themselves. In addition, healthy self-esteem reinforces good friendships and meaningful relationships by encouraging individuals to relate well with others without relying on them for approval or validation. Therefore, having a healthy level of self-esteem is essential for our overall well-being; it gives us the courage to take risks while remaining grounded in our true worth and identity. However, when it comes to life experiences such as trauma or hardship, it can be difficult for many of us to understand the emotions and struggles that a person may be going through. Therefore, it is crucial to recognise the diversity of experiences and empathise with those facing hardships. By understanding the perspectives of those who have endured these difficult times, we can gain insight into how trauma has shaped their lives and how they overcame their challenges. Through this understanding, we can build more compassionate communities and support systems, providing a safe and secure environment for individuals to heal and thrive.

***How good self-esteem can help us make decisions, interact with others, and take on new challenges***

High self-esteem helps us to feel confident and secure. This can help us make decisions more confidently, interact with others without fear or judgement, and take on new challenges, such as starting a business or learning a new skill. Developing good self-esteem means understanding our strengths and weaknesses and being honest with ourselves. *An accurate assessment of who we are can give us the courage to try something different, make changes that can improve our lives, and increase our confidence when interacting with others.* With increased self-esteem, we will be more likely to choose positive options for ourselves, such as taking up hobby activities that bring joy, rather than engaging in activities that may be damaging, like harmful behaviours or unhealthy relationships. We can better handle situations outside our control, rather than being overwhelmed by powerlessness, increasing our emotional resilience, mental health, and satisfaction with life. All these benefits combined lead to stronger emotional resilience, improved mental health, and greater life satisfaction. Having strong self-esteem is essential for leading a life of purpose and fulfilment. Having a secure and confident understanding of ourselves can help us take on new challenges and make decisions with more certainty. By recognising our strengths and weaknesses, being honest about them, and taking on new challenges, we can all make strides towards developing a firm and positive sense of self.

Sometimes, nearly everyone has low self-esteem. Negative feedback from others or one's evaluations of oneself can both contribute to feelings of low self-esteem. It tends to happen every so often. Unfortunately, for far too many people, poor self-esteem is an ever-present companion. This is especially true for those who struggle with mood disorders, anxiety, phobias, psychosis, hallucinations, or physical or mental impairments. Some people may go through life with an unwarranted sense of shame if they are one of these types. If you lack confidence in yourself, you won't be able to pursue the things that bring you happiness or move closer to achieving your objectives.

Low self-esteem can significantly impact a person's lifestyle and quality of life. It can cause feelings of sadness, inadequacy, hopelessness, and isolation. People with low self-esteem may also feel like they are not good enough for anyone or anything. These feelings can lead to an inability to take risks or try new things, difficulty forming relationships, and dissatisfaction with life. Low self-esteem can also manifest in physical or mental health symptoms such as sleep disturbances or changes in appetite or energy levels.

If you're having trouble enjoying life and making progress towards your objectives because of low self-esteem, know that you can take action to change your perspective.

Start by recognising the thoughts and beliefs that contribute to your negative thinking patterns and make a conscious effort to challenge them. Everyone has strengths and weaknesses - focus on what makes you unique and use that knowledge to build your confidence. Make a point of spending time doing things that bring you joy so you can better appreciate the value of your own experiences. Finally, seek support from friends, family members, therapy professionals, or support groups, so you do not have to go through this process alone.

Existing research indicates that women may face stereotype danger during mixed-gender discussions. However, nothing is known about the effect's boundary conditions. Scholars discovered a negative interaction impact of self-esteem level on socially contingent self-esteem in the stereotype threat scenario. (LU, Serena Changhong, 2015).

# Women and Threat Theory

*Negotiation* is where gender inequities in organisations are built and possibly dismantled (Bowles & McGinn, 2008). According to qualitative evaluations and meta-analyses, males do much better in economic negotiations than women (Kray & Thompson, 2005; Stuhlmacher & Walters, 1999). To explain gender variations in negotiation results, scholars often use the stereotype *threat theory*. When female negotiators face stereotype danger, a circumstance in which they believe they are at risk of confirming unfavourable preconceptions about their social group (Inzlicht & Schmader, 2012) - they achieve lower economic negotiating results (Kray & Thompson, 2005). In some instances, women's negotiating payoffs have been shown to meet or surpass men's payoffs. This shows that circumstances are essential: features of the person or setting mitigate the stereotype danger for female negotiators (Kray & Thompson, 2005).

Researchers investigated person-centred features to understand better when and why women negotiators confirm gender stereotype threats. They expanded the previous study by investigating the impact of self-esteem (SE). SE is a person's assessment of his or her self-worth - the degree to which individuals see themselves as good, competent, and decent (Harter, 1990) - and is one of the most effective predictors of people's behaviour (Pyszczynski et al., 2004).

As proposed by the self-consistency hypothesis (Korman, 1970; Swann Jr., Rentfrow, & Guinn, 2003), people with high SE are motivated to maintain an identity consistent with their positive self-evaluations.

In line with this, we contend that high SE women are driven to validate their favourable self-evaluations by achieving high performance in mixed-gender discussions. Scholars have also said that SE level and SE contingencies should be considered to fully understand SE effects (Crocker & Wolfe, 2001). As a result, researchers look at contingent social self-esteem (SCSE), which is defined as whether an individual's SE is reliant on the social acceptance of others (Crocker & Wolfe, 2001). They also contend that the favourable impact of SE level occurs only when women's SCSE is low. These predictions provide a complex model that combines two SE components to hypothesise SE's function in reducing stereotype threat in women's negotiations.

The researchers claim that when both SE level and SCSE are high, women will comply with gender role expectations regardless of SE level, resulting in gender stereotype reinforcement. Low SCSE women, on the other hand, are less concerned about possible criticism from others when they act contrary to gender standards, demonstrating the SE level's beneficial influence. When a stereotype threat is present during a negotiation, SE level and SCSE work together to affect the results, with a positive relationship between SE level and results when SCSE is low and a negative relationship when SCSE is high.(LU, Serena Changhong, 2015).

*How building self-esteem helps us become resilient when faced with difficult situations.*

Failure is unavoidable in life, but that does not make it any less terrible when it occurs. It may be complicated to deal with setbacks in your twenties and thirties since this is the first time many of us are experiencing significant 'failures,' such as not performing well in university or not getting the job you wanted.

Evidence shows that feeling like a failure increases the risk of depression, which could significantly affect mental health. This, in turn, may set off a negative feedback cycle, with depressed people more likely to focus on their failures and see themselves as failures.

While failure can be a severe issue, it is essential to remember that it comes with a lesson. Taking the time to reflect on a situation can help us better understand why it happened and see how we can use what we have learnt to improve. It is also essential to stay optimistic and talk to friends and family when dealing with failure. Having people who understand what you're going through and support you during this period can make all the difference. From seeking professional help, if needed, to actively looking for ways to improve, even a small step towards regaining control over your life may be enough to decrease depression symptoms. Taking responsibility for our failures is also essential without unnecessarily blaming ourselves. Rather than seeing these setbacks as personal failures, try to think of them as a learning experiences that can help you grow as an individual. Failure should not be seen as something inevitable but rather as something that could further stimulate growth and success in the long run.

Building self-esteem helps us become resilient when faced with difficult situations because having a healthy sense of self-worth gives us the courage and confidence to tackle challenging tasks. It is easier to face demanding tasks knowing we can develop the skills and strategies needed to overcome them. Additionally, having self-esteem gives us the belief

When faced with a difficult situation, having self-esteem allows us to believe that we have what it takes to handle it. This can be empowering, giving us the confidence to tackle the challenge without feeling overwhelmed or discouraged. With the belief that we can handle whatever comes our way, we are more likely to approach complex tasks with a positive attitude and the willingness to take risks. Having self-esteem also means that when things do not go as planned, we do not see it as a failure but as a learning opportunity. We can use these setbacks to gain valuable insight into our capabilities and shortcomings to grow and develop more effectively. In this way, having a healthy sense of self-worth helps us become resilient when faced with challenging situations, giving us the strength and determination to persist despite the opposition.

Building self-esteem is essential to becoming resilient when faced with difficult situations. Self-esteem is our evaluation of ourselves, and it determines how we handle ourselves, cope with challenges, and accept criticism. When we have healthy self-esteem, we have a strong sense of worthiness and acceptance.

So, we are more willing to try new things, trust our judgement, and be open to new experiences. This helps us to become more resilient because we can face challenging situations with optimism instead of fear or self-doubt.

When we have high self-worth, we may call on our inner fortitude to keep going even when things are tough.

We are also better equipped to handle criticism or failure without feeling overwhelmed or defeated. Overall, building a healthy level of self-esteem is essential for developing resilience and bouncing back from any setbacks that life throws our way.

Self-esteem is an essential component of resilience. When we have healthy self-esteem, we are more likely to take risks, make decisions confidently, and be open to new experiences. This helps us become more resilient because we can face challenging situations with optimism and draw on our inner strength. Additionally, having strong self-esteem allows us to handle criticism or failure without feeling overwhelmed or defeated.

If we want to boost our confidence, we need to take stock of our successes and accomplishments, view our setbacks as learning experiences, and have an optimistic outlook no matter how difficult things become. With a strong sense of worthiness and acceptance of ourselves as individuals, we can become more resilient and better equipped to handle the adversities life throws our way.

## Developing Strategies to Build Self-Esteem

Developing a strategy to help build self-esteem can take time and effort, even for experienced professionals. It requires an understanding and appreciation of the individual's unique qualities, likes and dislikes, values, strengths, weaknesses and developmental needs.

The individual's existing outlook and way of life are both factors that must be considered while formulating an effective plan of action.

The first step in developing strategies to build self-esteem is identifying areas of low self-esteem that need improvement. This can be done by talking with the individual and observing their behaviour. Once these areas have been identified, providing supportive feedback and positive reinforcement is essential whenever possible. Additionally, providing opportunities for individuals to set realistic goals and achieve them can help boost their confidence in their capabilities. Creating an environment that encourages healthy communication and problem-solving is also essential. This means providing support during challenging moments while allowing individuals to express themselves freely without fear of criticism or judgement. Additionally, teaching practical, emotional regulation skills can help them manage times when they may feel overwhelmed or frustrated due to their perceived lack of success or ability.

## *The importance of positive self-talk*

Positive self-talk is a powerful tool to increase self-confidence and build inner strength. It involves regularly reminding yourself of your strengths, capabilities, and successes instead of focusing on your weaknesses or mistakes. Positive self-talk helps to counter negative thoughts and can help you make better decisions in difficult situations. In addition, it demonstrates that you have faith in yourself and your abilities and motivates you to achieve your goals.

It can help you relax, learn about your unique requirements, and ultimately make better choices. Regular positive affirmations make it easier to take risks and push out of our comfort zone, leading to more outstanding achievements. Positive self-talk can improve mental health, helping us feel better about ourselves and our lives and strengthening our relationships with others. Practising positive self-talk is essential for improved mental health and well-being. As we learn to talk in a more kind, understanding and compassionate way to ourselves, it can help us cultivate a healthier relationship with our inner thoughts and beliefs. This can lead to improved self-esteem and better relationships with others as our mental well-being improves. Positive self-talk can also help strengthen our resolve in difficult times, providing much-needed support and motivation when things seem too hard. By replacing negative self-talk with statements of affirmation and encouragement, we can shift our mindset in a more positive direction and build healthier habits that benefit our mental health.

### *Practice self-care and set boundaries*

Self-care and setting boundaries are essential to create a sense of well-being and balance in life. It is important to practice self-care as it allows us to take care of our physical and mental health. Engaging in activities such as exercise, healthy eating, meditation, or getting adequate sleep can help us feel more energised and better able to face life's challenges. Additionally, it gives us time to focus on ourselves, allowing us the space to recognise and appreciate whom we are, further strengthening our sense of self-worth. Setting boundaries is also crucial in achieving a healthy balance in life. Having clear boundaries helps protect our energy, time, and resources by enabling us to decide where we focus our attention and effort. When we set boundaries, we are putting into action what is important to us while being mindful not to overextend ourselves due to the demands of others or other external factors. By establishing firm yet respectful boundaries, we can ensure that our needs are met without violating the rights of others.

When it comes to establishing boundaries and respecting the rights of others, it is essential to be aware of one's limits and those of others. By taking the time to consider our needs and those of others, we can ensure that healthy boundaries are set and respected. This means taking the time to listen and understand how each person's individual needs may differ from another's. Additionally, taking responsibility for our feelings and reactions is vital rather than blaming them on someone else.

It is crucial to be specific when laying out rules regarding what is and is not allowed.

Being assertive when setting boundaries is also essential, as a lack of clarity can lead to misunderstandings or conflicts. Furthermore, it is essential to remember that everyone has their own set of boundaries that must be respected and honoured. Ultimately, by working together to establish firm yet respectful boundaries, we can ensure that our needs are met without violating the rights of others.

### *Spend time with positive people*

Spending time with positive people can be beneficial for a variety of reasons. Being around those who have an optimistic outlook and choose to see the good in any situation can lift the spirits of those around them, making it easier to stay positive, even during difficult times. Additionally, spending time with positive people can have a contagious effect, and observing their optimism makes it possible to learn how to think and act more positively. When surrounded by upbeat people, you are more likely to participate in activities that bring joy or engage in conversations that promote creative problem-solving rather than fear-based thinking. This can open up new possibilities, create opportunities for personal growth, and help us gain insight into different perspectives we may not have otherwise encountered. We can often benefit from their mentorship and coaching by spending time with positive people while feeling uplifted. Spending time with positive people is a great way to benefit from their mentorship and coaching while feeling uplifted at the same time. Positive people bring a sense of joy and enthusiasm that can be contagious, and their words of encouragement can help give us the courage to tackle complex or challenging tasks. With their input and guidance, we can develop our skills and abilities, gain new perspectives on life, and reach our goals. Positive mentors can help us stay motivated, confident, and inspired in times of difficulty while providing us with the wisdom and experience we need to make good decisions. By encountering those who are positive, we can discover new ways of thinking that can allow us to create meaningful and lasting change in our lives.

### *Push yourself beyond established boundaries.*

It is easy to become comfortable with the everyday routine of life, but that can lead to stagnation and a lack of growth. Breaking out of your comfort zone requires taking calculated risks, pushing past your boundaries, and challenging yourself in ways that may initially be uncomfortable. This process is beneficial because it helps you grow and encourages personal development in self-confidence, problem-solving, creativity, and resilience. Taking the time to step outside of what we know leads to more excellent knowledge and understanding of the world around us. As a result, you become more capable of adapting to new situations and handling unforeseen obstacles.

Additionally, pushing yourself beyond what's familiar can help break bad habits and open up new career opportunities or experiences. Ultimately, taking the initiative to challenge yourself allows for enhanced learning capabilities and improved mental strength, leading to increased success in all areas of life. Taking the initiative is an important skill to develop in any situation.

It's human nature to want to pursue the path of least resistance when faced with adversity. However, when facing a challenge, we are forced to think outside the box, build problem-solving skills, and use our creativity to develop innovative solutions. In addition, taking the initiative helps us to develop valuable skills such as time management, organisation, and resourcefulness that are essential for achieving success. Ultimately, taking the initiative to face and overcome challenges can help us reach our goals and maximise our potential.

Good self-esteem is essential for living a happy and meaningful life. It is the foundation from which we make decisions, interact with others, and take on new challenges. It can also help us to become resilient when faced with difficult situations. Of course, developing a healthy sense of self-worth isn't always a walk in the park, but it's crucial to your overall development.

## In a Nutshell

*Self-Esteem* can be defined as an individual's subjective evaluation of their worth. It is a cognitive construct that reflects the appraisal of one's positive or negative self-concept based on perceived successes and failures in various domains of life. Self-esteem is believed to be underpinned by various psychological mechanisms, such as attributions, feedback loops, and affective responses, as well as social comparison processes. It has been theorised as a multi-dimensional construct of global self-worth, perceived competence, and perceived attractiveness. Self-esteem can be positive and negative, influencing a person's behaviours, emotions and relationships.

*Developing Self-Love* is something that many people struggle with, especially in a society that tends to emphasise physical appearance and success. However, Self-love is being kind and compassionate towards oneself, which can help build self-esteem and create healthy relationships with the world around us. Every person has unique strengths, talents, and experiences that should be appreciated and celebrated. With a little effort, anyone can learn how to develop self-love. However, it requires a commitment to taking time for yourself regularly and understanding what you need emotionally, physically, mentally and spiritually to thrive. Start by identifying any negative thought patterns or beliefs about yourself - then take steps to discover what it means for you to truly love yourself by exploring activities like yoga or meditation.

*Understanding Self-Worth* is an essential step towards building self-esteem. It's a process that involves looking at yourself, recognising your strengths and weaknesses, and developing an understanding of who you are as a person. Self-worth is the foundation upon which self-esteem is built; once you have developed an appreciation for yourself, it will become easier to create positive feelings about your actions. The key to understanding self-worth is to focus on being kind to yourself. It's important not to let negative thoughts creep in when evaluating yourself - instead, focus on your accomplishments and what makes you unique. This can be done through journaling or reflecting on who you are and what brings joy. Learning to appreciate oneself allows for higher confidence levels and will enable us to celebrate our successes more fully.

*Setting Reasonable Goals* is a crucial factor in building self-esteem. Plans can be broken down into short-term, mid-term and long-term objectives. When setting these goals, it is vital to make sure they are achievable in an appropriate amount of time. When striving to reach a goal, individuals should ensure their expectations are realistic and attainable. For example, if someone wants to lose weight, they should set smaller targets, such as losing one pound per week instead of attempting to lose ten pounds daily. These incremental steps will help them reach the larger goal without becoming discouraged or overwhelmed by the task. In addition, having rewards for meeting each benchmark can provide additional motivation and help keep one on track with reaching their end goal.

*Practising Positive Thinking* is integral to building self-esteem and improving mental health. Recognising and reversing negative thinking patterns contributing to low self-esteem requires active and conscious effort. Practising positive thinking can help individuals develop a more optimistic outlook, boost confidence, and deal with difficult emotions. Achieving positivity begins by recognising the automatic negative thoughts that may creep up throughout the day. By becoming conscious of these destructive patterns in thinking, individuals can better address the source of such anxieties or worries rather than letting them fester in their minds. In addition, once they become aware of what triggers these negative thoughts, they can work on strategies to reframe those situations in a more productive light. Developing a daily journaling practice or mindfulness can be a helpful tool for mastering positive thinking techniques.

*Seeking Support and Encouragement* when building self-esteem can be challenging to do alone. Seeking support and encouragement from friends, family members, or even professionals is a great way to help. Feeling supported by people who care about us and having our accomplishments recognised makes us feel more confident in our abilities. Everyone needs some support network, whether leaning on close relationships with those we trust, finding an online community of like-minded individuals or seeing a therapist. Through understanding and validation of what we're going through, these relationships can provide comfort and help ease any feelings of loneliness or isolation that may arise. This boosts self-esteem and allows for better problem-solving skills when faced with difficult situations. Creating a safe space for ourselves to receive positive reinforcement is essential for gaining confidence in ourselves and our decisions.

*Adopting Healthy Habits* is a great way to build self-esteem. So many people struggle with issues of low self-worth, and developing good habits can help combat those feelings. From eating nutritious meals and exercising regularly to getting enough sleep and taking time, there are many ways to start forming positive habits to help you feel better about yourself. The key is to start small and set achievable goals that you know you can accomplish. For example, set the alarm five minutes earlier than usual so you can take the time for a morning stretch or walk around the block. Then gradually increase the amount of exercise as it becomes more comfortable. Eating healthier foods can also be tackled in small steps; try replacing your sugary snacks with fruits or vegetables, then progress from there.

### *Conclusion: Embracing Self-Confidence*

Believing in oneself is essential to self-esteem, and building a positive attitude starts with embracing self-confidence. It is necessary to understand that we all have unique abilities, strengths and weaknesses. With the right mindset and dedication to self-improvement, anyone can learn to accept themselves and become more confident.

Self-confidence is the key to unlocking our potential. It allows us to take risks, try new things and make mistakes without fear of failure or judgment from others. Confidence in ourselves gives us the courage to pursue our goals and dreams without hesitation or worrying about what other people think. Gaining self-confidence requires practice, but with hard work, dedication and patience, anyone can become more secure in their abilities.

- *On the importance of building self-esteem for personal growth and development*

In the end, personal growth and development need to have a healthy sense of self-worth. It gives people the courage to try new things, express themselves, and move forward, even if they fail or face problems. Knowing one's value helps one make choices that get one closer to one's dreams and ambitions. Building one's self-esteem also allows one to embrace unique qualities, which helps build strong relationships with others. Lastly, people with higher self-esteem can better figure out their goals and work toward them with clarity and purpose. This helps them be more successful in life.

- *About the power of believing in yourself*

When we believe in ourselves, it can unlock our potential for success and happiness. Self-belief is essential for achieving goals and living our best lives. It gives us confidence in our decisions, taking risks, and making positive changes to enhance our life experiences. With self-belief, we can overcome challenges and learn from mistakes without feeling demoralised or hopeless. When we have faith in ourselves, we can face adversity with the fortitude and hope that will carry us through. Believing in ourselves empowers us to create a better future where we can reach our full potential.

- *Working on developing self-esteem is an*

*ongoing process*

Developing self-esteem is an ongoing process that takes time and effort. It cannot be done in a single day but requires consistent effort over an extended period. An individual should remember that sometimes progress may be slow, but this does not mean it is not worthwhile or achievable. Working on activities such as setting goals, completing tasks, building relationships and engaging in self-reflection are all critical steps to boosting one's self-esteem. Additionally, avoiding negative influences and focusing on positive affirmations can help boost one's morale and reinforce self-esteem. Ultimately, developing high self-esteem is learning to accept and value oneself and recognising one's worth.

### Key-recommendations

1. Start a daily affirmation journal where you can

write down all the good things about yourself and your goals.

2. Set yourself achievable goals and celebrate when you achieve them.

3. Identify activities that bring you joy, and schedule some time for them every week.

4. Make time for yourself by engaging in activities such as yoga, meditation, or taking a relaxing bath.

5. Make a list of people who make you feel good about yourself and make an effort to surround yourself with them.

6. Create a personal mantra or phrase you can remind yourself of whenever you feel down.

7. Make a "kindness jar"—write down compliments or affirmations that you have received or positive thoughts about yourself, and put them in the jar to remind yourself of them whenever necessary.

8. Once you recognise negative thoughts about yourself, try positively reframing them.

9. Dedicate time to self-reflection and figuring out your values and passions.

10. Write down one thing you achieve each day, no matter how small, to remind yourself of your progress.

# 3 - The Modern Spiritual Challenge of Personal Development

*It takes a Herculean effort to grow spiritually in a society where power, money, and influence are the most important things. But on the other hand, electronic equipment, gadgets, tools, and entertainment like TV, magazines, and the internet have taught us to pay attention to our bodies and what they need and want. As a consequence, our ideas about self-worth and self-meaning have become jumbled. So, how can we find a happy medium between our material and spiritual selves?*

Balancing our material and spiritual selves can seem daunting in a society that places so much importance on power, money, and influence. With the multitude of electronic gadgets, tools, and entertainment available to us, it is easy to become distracted by the pursuit of physical gratification. We are taught that we must strive to satisfy our needs to succeed. This can lead us to forget our spiritual self and its need for nourishment through meaningful experiences, relationships, and activities. To find a happy medium between the two aspects of our lives, we must keep ourselves grounded in both the material and spiritual realms. We need to be mindful of how much time we spend pursuing physical gratification versus engaging with activities that bring us joy or contribute positively towards our emotional well-being. Additionally, being open-minded about exploring different spiritual practices, such as meditation or mindfulness, can help us develop a deeper understanding of ourselves. Finally, it is critical to remember that by attempting to nurture both material and spiritual aspects of ourselves, we can achieve greater harmony within ourselves.

***To develop spiritually, one must search inside.***

Introspection extends beyond remembering events from the previous day, week, or month. It would help if you examined your ideas, emotions, beliefs, and motives. Reading your experiences, choices, relationships, and activities regularly may give important insights into your life objectives, the positive attributes you must maintain, and the undesirable ones you must reject. Furthermore, it guides how to behave, respond, and conduct oneself in each scenario. Introspection, like any ability, can be learnt; all that is required is bravery and commitment to exploring the truths inside you. Here are some things to consider while looking back: Be realistic, forgive yourself, and concentrate on your areas for progress.

Introspection is about looking back into your past and considering what you can do in the future. It demands contemplation of how to change and grow as a person. Constructive ways one can benefit from examining their life include setting achievable goals, exploring dreams, breaking down any obstacles that may hinder growth, and discovering ways to express yourself better. Knowing how to utilise introspection exercises allows individuals to become more aware of themselves and how they think, feel, and act. *To stay spiritually enlightened, one should invest in activities that nurture understanding and self-realisation, such as meditation, journaling, creative art expression and spiritual readings.* Regular practice allows introspection to foster personal growth while developing a greater appreciation for self-discovery.

## Growing spiritually means realising your full potential.

Religion and science have opposing viewpoints on the human spirit. Faith sees people as spiritual beings temporarily living on Earth, but science considers the spirit as just one part of a person. Self-mastery is common in Christian (Western) and Islamic (Eastern) teachings. The needs of the body are considered, but they come after the needs of the soul. Beliefs, values, morals, laws, experiences, and good actions give the pattern for spiritual development. In psychology, self-actualisation is defined as attaining one's full potential.

Growing spiritually does not mean believing in faith or following the teachings of a religion. Instead, it is about finding harmony with your environment and discovering who you indeed are. It involves finding a balance between faith and science, between the spiritual and the physical. Through this balance, we can better understand our place in the world and our relationship with others. Achieving self-actualisation involves personal growth through learning, developing good habits, and incorporating principles from both religion and science. By engaging in activities that support our mental, spiritual and physical well-being such as meditation, prayer or exercise; by observing our behaviours thoughtfully; by setting realistic goals for ourselves; by being open to new experiences; and by striving to live a life of service to others, we can focus on achieving a deeper understanding of ourselves and attain our fullest potential.

Abraham Maslow, a prominent psychologist, proposed in two seminal works (1943, 1954) that the driving force behind human behaviour is the pursuit of self-actualisation. Maslow defined various human wants, including physiological, safety, belonging, esteem, cognitive, aesthetic, self-actualisation, and self-transcendence. Maslow famously proposed a hierarchy of needs, in which the basic physiological needs such as food, water and warmth must be met before higher-level needs such as love and belonging are achieved. Once physiological conditions have been satisfied, humans can focus on safety; once safety is taken care of, people can concentrate on belonging; once belonging is provided for, esteem can become a priority, followed by cognitive needs like knowledge and understanding; then aesthetic needs such as beauty and balance; progressing to self-actualisation – the need to achieve one's full potential – and finally the need for self-transcendence – the realisation that we are all connected. According to Maslow, these human wants form a staircase that we climb until we reach our highest potential. (Maslow's Hierarchy of Needs, By Saul Mcleod, 2007).

In *The Principles of Psychology,* William James (1890) says our emotions must always be inwardly what they are, whatever the physiological ground of their apparition if they are deep, pure, worthy, and spiritual. James classified the above demands as material, emotional, and spiritual. After you've taken care of your basic physical and emotional needs, you can pay attention to your spiritual or existential needs. The fulfilment of each condition leads to the natural growth of the person. Perhaps the most significant distinction between these two faiths and psychology is the goal of self-development: Christianity and Islam consider self-development as a means to an end of serving God, while psychology sees self-development as an end in and of itself. James proposed that to reach a state of well-being, there were three basic categories of needs to be fulfilled: material, emotional and spiritual. Material needs are those related to one's physical health and safety. They include food, clothing and shelter. Emotional needs are those related to feeling secure, loved and appreciated. These can be met through relationships with others as well as participation in activities that make us feel good. Spiritual needs include having a sense of purpose or meaning in life, which can be found through religious faith or other forms of personal exploration such as art, music or philosophy. The fundamental difference between Christianity, Islam and psychology is the goal of self-development. These two faiths view it as a means to serve God (and ultimately attain salvation), while psychology views self-development as an end in itself. Therefore, fulfilling these three conditions – material, emotional and spiritual – leads to natural growth in all areas of one's life, enabling one to reach greater levels of well-being and mental health.

*Spiritual development entails a quest for meaning.*

Religions that believe in God, such as Christianity, Judaism, and Islam, believe that the goal of human life is to serve the Creator of all things. Several psychological theories contend that we eventually provide meaning to our lives. Whether we feel that the purpose of life is predetermined or self-directed, growing in spirit means realising that we do not just exist. We may not know the significance of our existence when we are born, but we learn and grow through our relationships with others and our actions and responses to the circumstances we find ourselves in. We reject and support particular ideas and ideals as we uncover this meaning. Our lives have sense. This purpose utilises all of our physical, emotional, and intellectual abilities; it supports us through difficult times and provides us with something to look forward to—-a goal to attain, a destination to reach. A person who lacks purpose or meaning is like a ship at sea.

To discover this purpose, individuals must engage in spiritual development. They need to practice self-awareness, look inward, and become aware of the thoughts they are thinking, the feelings they are having, and the beliefs they are embracing. Whether their source of guidance comes from a higher power or another individual, people should strive to develop inner peace and live with integrity. This calls for making good choices that align with one's values and beliefs. Additionally, meditation can help us to recognise an inner truth and open our hearts to that truth. Finally, we must maintain an attitude of gratitude. We often forget how fortunate we are until something goes wrong in our lives; this is why a resilient attitude of thankfulness is so crucial for our spiritual development.

We must create our spiritual compass and set sail. The quest for meaning in life is an essential aspect of spiritual development. This can manifest itself in various ways, depending on the religion or faith that one follows.

It is believed in Christianity, Judaism, and Islam that God has a purpose for every one of us and that our role is to serve Him.

However, many psychological theories suggest that we have the freedom to choose our paths in life and ultimately create the meanings of our existence. This involves continuously learning from both positive and negative experiences in life, developing strong relationships with people around us and choosing which values, beliefs and ideas we want to adopt. Having a sense of purpose also helps to motivate us and gives us something to strive for; it gives direction to our lives when facing difficult times - An accurate spiritual compass!

In the end, it depends on each person. To find their purpose, but being aware along the way will help them get through life's storms.

We must make our spiritual compass and set sail on the path to self-discovery, inner peace, and the real meaning of life. To do this, we must start by taking a step back from our everyday lives and begin to explore the inner workings of our minds. We must start to ask thoughtful questions about life and look for answers that come from within. Energise our thoughts around the possibilities of achieving true happiness and joy in life through self-reflection and inner exploration. As we take these steps, we should be mindful of our environment, relationships, and the people closest to us. We can use these relationships as learning tools to understand ourselves further and move closer towards defining our purpose in life. We can also draw upon the wisdom of others whose experiences might help guide us along the way. Through conversations with friends, colleagues, mentors, or even strangers, we can gain valuable insight into different paths that lead to spiritual growth. Every journey has its highs and lows; however, it's important to remember that setbacks are only temporary if faced with an open mind. Use those moments as an opportunity to reflect on successes achieved so far and adjust your spiritual compass accordingly. With each discovery comes a greater understanding of oneself—an understanding that's beneficial not only for you but for those around you too.

## Spiritual development entails seeing links.

Religions emphasise our interconnectedness with all of creation, both living and inanimate. As a result, we refer to others as "brothers and sisters" even if they are not biological relatives—furthermore, deity-centred faiths such as Christianity and Islam talk of humans' connection with a higher entity. On the other hand, science elaborates on our connection to other living things via evolution. This similarity is evident in ecology, which refers to the interplay of living and non-living entities. In psychology, the connection is a quality of self-transcendence, Maslow's ultimate human need. Recognising your interconnectedness with all things makes you more modest and appreciative of people, animals, plants, and natural phenomena. It helps you appreciate your surroundings. It inspires you to go beyond your comfort zone, reach out to others, and become stewards of everything around you.

Because spiritual growth is a process, it is something that happens daily. We win some, we lose some, but the essential thing is that we learn, and this information allows for future spiritual progress. Spiritual development requires developing an appreciation for the interconnectedness of all things that comprise our universe. This interconnectedness is highlighted in religions such as Christianity and Islam, where humans are connected to a higher entity, while science explains our connection to other living things via evolution. This idea of the interplay between living and non-living entities is also evident in ecology. In psychology, this connection is expressed as a quality of self-transcendence, which Maslow identified as an essential human need. Reconciling this interconnectedness can result in greater humility and gratitude for the people, animals, plants and natural phenomena around us. In addition, by recognising our interconnectedness with these things, we are inspired to reach out beyond our comfort zones and take on the responsibility of stewardship towards our environment. Spiritual growth can be seen as a continuing process that occurs daily within us; it is through these experiences that we gain knowledge which will help drive our spiritual progress forward. There may be times when we have successes or setbacks, but we need to accept those experiences and keep progressing on the path of spiritual growth.

## Unleashing your potential

*Why does it matter to unlock potential, and*

### *what is potential?*

Individuals frequently underestimate their potential and the heights of which they are capable. *When we compare where we are now to where we might be, that's our potential. When a person has potential, they usually achieve their goals.* It's not about success per se (although, for many, this is precisely what it is). Finding inner calm is a primary goal for some. Being, rather than possessing or doing, is the focus for some. For others, it's about establishing meaningful connections with people and expressing their unique selves. Unlocking potential involves understanding our aptitudes and values. This helps us focus on the tasks that are meaningful and important to us without getting bogged down in those that are not. Our abilities tell us what skills we need to work on and how we can put them to good use. Our values tell us what's most important to us, so we can put activities at the top of the list that fits our sense of purpose. To reach these goals, we need to work hard and be committed, but we also need to know what we can do and how strong we are. When we realise our potential, we unlock a new confidence level within ourselves. We become aware of our strengths, weaknesses, and possibilities for growth. This helps us put our actions in order of importance so that they support the things we care about most. Through discovering our potential comes an acknowledgement of who we are as individuals and how far we can go. We can break free from self-doubt and fear of failure by recognising that anything is possible when effort is combined with belief in ourselves. Unlocking our potential drives us to take charge of our lives and go beyond what we thought was possible.

Some could argue that the very fact that we have to tell you to "Unleash Your Potential" shows that something is wrong with you or that you're not good enough the way you are. But, from where individuals are, I want to assist them in reaching their full potential and accomplishing their goals and ambitions. The goal is to help people get past whatever stops them from reaching their life goals.

Unlocking your potential for self-improvement starts with realising that you can make changes in your life that matter. It is about owning your development journey and being intentional about how you want to grow. While we cannot influence many external things in our surroundings, we can manage our thoughts, feelings, and behaviours. We can decide how best to use our time, energy, and resources to achieve our goals. By becoming mindful of our thoughts and attitudes, we can use them to our advantage rather than letting them hold us back from reaching our full potential. Recognising how past experiences shape current beliefs helps us identify how we might become better versions of ourselves now and in the future. Examining these patterns can help us create more effective strategies for success in any area of life: work, relationships, finances, or personal growth. Additionally, by studying the habits and practices of successful people who have achieved success before us - such as entrepreneurs, athletes, or artists - we can gain insight into powerful

But if we push it a bit more, we'll get a better picture of the whole piece. The same is true with oneself. We often do so from a very close range when we look at ourselves or observe our thoughts and feelings. When appreciating the bigger picture, seeing what is happening underneath the surface can be challenging and even complicated. But if we take a step back and look at ourselves from a distance, we can start to see the patterns that emerge in our lives, gain insight into our motivations and emotions, and even better understand why certain events have happened in our past. By seeing further away than just up close, we better understand our perspectives on life, allowing us to grow emotionally and intellectually.

We reach a time when we are ready for change and have a slew of knowledge to help us unleash our self-improvement potential. Something may be glaring at us until then, but we are blind to it. We only consider unlocking our self-improvement potential when things are bad. The dictum goes that you only sense bushes once you tread on them. Once we realise how much we can improve ourselves, figuring out how to do it can be scary. We feel overwhelmed by the sheer number of available resources and need a direction or plan to help us use them effectively. Sometimes it seems we're the blind man searching for a black cat in a room full of light.

This can lead to frustration and discouragement, which can further impede progress. To maximise our self-improvement potential, we must find a way to make sense of what's available. It could mean asking for help from mentors or coaches who have been there before. With their guidance and support, you can understand what works best for you and determine steps for achieving your goals through careful planning and execution. Additionally, it's essential to take time out for yourself throughout this journey - whether it's taking regular breaks from work or simply going on vacation once in a while - so that you don't get bogged down with the effort that self-improvement requires. Self-care is essential for reaching your full potential!

When we are in agony, we learn our lessons. When

things become dire, we finally recognise the warning signs and signals. When do we know we need to adjust our diet? When our pants and shirts don't fit. When do we quit eating chocolate and candy? When we've lost all of our teeth. When do we understand we have to quit smoking? When our lungs have failed us. When do we pray and seek assistance? When we know we're going to die tomorrow.

Most of us only learn about accessing our self-improvement power when the world collapses. We think and feel this way because change is difficult. However, ignoring change makes it more unpleasant.

The change will occur, whether you like it or not. We will all encounter various turning points in our lives at some time, and we will finally unlock our self-improvement power not because the world says so, not because our friends are pestering us, but because we understand it was for our benefit.

People who are happy welcome change rather than tolerate it. You no longer need to experience extreme heat to recognise the need for self-improvement. *Freeing your self-improvement power entails unlocking yourself from the prison of the idea that "this is simply the way I am".* It's a terrible reason for people to be afraid of and reject change. Most of us programme our thoughts in the same way that computers do.

Happy people understand that change is inevitable and welcome it as an opportunity for improvement. Instead of simply tolerating it, they use change as a catalyst to grow positively. They recognise that although some changes may feel difficult or uncomfortable initially, they can ultimately lead to growth and enlightenment. The idea that we must experience extreme conditions to motivate ourselves no longer applies. We can free our inner power of self-improvement by breaking free from the idea that our current state is all we can ever be. In other words, people should not accept limitations on their potential to grow and improve continuously – even if it means letting go of old habits and beliefs. This type of thinking is similar to how computers programme their software – rather than accepting preset programming, we should look for opportunities to upgrade our 'software' through personal development activities like learning new skills or taking on a different exercise routine. This way, we are constantly improving, adapting and growing.

Lilian continually tells everyone that she lacks the courage to be around large gatherings of people. She had heard her mother, sister, and instructor say the same things about her to other people. Lilian has come to think about this over the years. She believes it's her narrative. What happens next? When a large crowd gathers at their home, school, or in the town, she tends to shrink back, hide away and shut herself in a room. Lilian not only believed in her tale, but she lived it. Although Lilian has had many people, including family members, confirm that she lacks courage, it doesn't mean that this is who she truly is. Whenever Lilian is around large gatherings of people, she tends to shrink back and hide away in a room. She does this because she believes the narrative about herself that has been told over the years. Lilian's behaviour reinforces her thoughts about herself and creates a vicious cycle where she continues to think and act as if she lacks courage or strength. However, deep down, Lilian knows that this isn't true. She understands that with practice and determination, she can change her story and become the confident person she longs to be. Rather than succumbing to fear and negativity every time a large gathering appears, Lilian will start to take steps towards positively changing her narrative by putting herself in difficult situations and pushing through challenging emotions whenever they come up. With patience and self-love each day, Lilian can find her inner strength and discover how courageous she really is. Not only did Lilian overcome her crowd phobia, but she also developed into a strong-minded industry leader under whose orders dozens of people work at the factory.

Self-improvement may not be everyone's favourite phrase. Still, if we look at things from a different perspective, we may have a better chance of enjoying the whole process rather than counting the days until we are entirely improved. For example, going to the gym three times a week will result in a healthier existence, reading books instead of watching porn will shape a more comprehensive knowledge, and going out with friends and peers will help you take a step back from work and decompress. And just as you're starting to appreciate the process of unleashing your self-improvement power, you'll notice that you're starting to lighten up and become happier. Self-improvement may sound like a tedious task that nobody wants to do, but if you look at it in a different light, it can be an enjoyable and rewarding experience. Doing small tasks such as going to the gym three times a week, reading books instead of watching porn, and socialising with friends and peers can all benefit your mental and physical well-being. As your efforts slowly take shape, you'll start feeling happier and better about yourself. Not only will you become healthier, more knowledgeable, and more relaxed, but you'll also find joy in pushing yourself to improve. Self-improvement can be an exciting journey of self-discovery that makes life much more fulfilling.

Keep in mind that self-improvement includes a wide range of aspects and activities. Here are a few details that deserve your attention:

- Determine what you want; if you dwell on the negative, more will pass. If you see obstacles, you will only encounter them. Remember your goals. "Anxiety is a message from the unconscious mind to concentrate on what you desire," as Tad James puts it. Don't let yourself get blown about like a rudderless ship at sea; choose a course. When setting and achieving goals, the key is to focus your energy on what you want. Worrying about things that could go wrong or roadblocks that might stop you from reaching your goal can be tempting. However, this kind of negative thinking won't get you anywhere. Instead, focus on the positive – what you want to gain and how you can get there. Don't let yourself be pushed around by whatever circumstance may come up – decide for yourself what direction you want to take in life and stick with it. Rather than being pulled along by the waves like a ship without a rudder, choose a course and put your efforts into making it happen.

- Try to get a sense of your talents and what you like doing since this will help you zero in on your areas of expertise. Keep your hobbies in check. Never underestimate the power of strength, enthusiasm, concentration, and tenacity. You should try to explore different areas of interest to find out which activities bring you the most joy and satisfaction. Identifying your talents will help you focus on the areas where you excel, and you will take pride in honing those skills.

- Having hobbies and interests outside of work is important, but ensure they do not distract from your goals or mental well-being. It is also essential to recognise how powerful determination, enthusiasm, focus, and resilience can be in achieving success. When faced with a difficult task or challenge, having these characteristics will motivate you to push forward and work through any obstacles to reach your goal. Working hard and never giving up are critical elements in realising your full potential and striving towards success.

- Be bold, put yourself out there, and take some chances; this is why individuals fail to achieve their objectives. Avoiding danger is counterproductive; instead, you should welcome it by venturing outside your safety net into the unknown, where genuine innovation may occur. The more you push yourself, even a little, you'll find that your comfort zone grows unexpectedly and that you reap benefits in previously unrelated aspects of your life.

- No matter what happens, there is no such thing as failure, just feedback (from which you may grow and improve). Take a leap of faith and be audacious; this is why people cannot accomplish their goals. Refrain from shying away from risks; instead, embrace the unknown for potential ground-breaking ideas. The further you dare to push your limits, the larger your comfort zone will become, offering various advantages in different areas of life.

- You can't find an unresourceful individual, just a state lacking resources. Emotional regulation is a skill that may be practised at any time (in fact, participants in our courses learn how to do it immediately). If you're the kind of person whose mood might change depending on the company they keep, put yourself in the company of positive thinkers and doers. Having the resources available to you and having the ability to use them are two different things, however. Just because an individual may lack or have limited access to specific resources doesn't mean they cannot make good use of what they do have. It simply means they must look for more creative solutions and alternative routes to achieving their goals.

- Emotional regulation is a skill that may be practised at any time. It involves choosing how we respond to something instead of automatically reacting in ways potentially putting us into negative emotional states. It is not necessarily instinctual; it needs to be learnt and developed so that individuals can effectively manage their emotions instead of allowing themselves to be emotionally controlled by external factors.

# Bibliography

***Introduction and Chapter One***

Psychological Perspectives on Self-Development, Psychoanalyst Sigmund Freud (1856–1939).

Cooley, Charles Horton. 1902. "The Looking Glass Self." Pp. 179–185 in Human Nature and Social Order. New York: Scribner's.

Bloom, Lisa. 2011. "How to Talk to Little Girls." Huffington Post, June 22. Retrieved January 12, 2012 (http://www.huffingtonpost.com/lisa-bloom/how-to-talk-to-little-gir_b_882510.html).

Erikson, Erik. 1982. The Lifecycle Completed: A

Review. New York: Norton.

Durkheim, Émile. 2011 [1897]. Suicide. London: Routledge.

Freud, Sigmund. 2000 [1904]. Three Essays on Theories of Sexuality. New York: Basic Books.

Gilligan, Carol. 1982. In a Different Voice: Psychological Theory and Women's Development. Cambridge, MA: Harvard University Press.

Gilligan, Carol. 1990. Making Connections: The Relational Worlds of Adolescent Girls at Emma Willard School. Cambridge, MA: Harvard University Press.

Haney, Phil. 2011. "Genderless Preschool in Sweden." Baby & Kids, June 28. Retrieved January 12, 2012 (http://www.neatorama.com/2011/06/28/genderle ss-preschool-in-sweden/).

Harlow, Harry F. 1971. Learning to Love. New York: Ballantine.

Harlow, Harry F., and Margaret Kuenne Harlow.

1962. "Social Deprivation in Monkeys." Scientific American November:137–46.

Kohlberg, Lawrence. 1981. The Psychology of Moral Development: The Nature and Validity of Moral Stages. New York: Harper and Row.

Mead, George H. 1934. Mind, Self and Society, edited by C. W. Morris. Chicago: University of Chicago Press.

Mead, George H. 1964. On Social Psychology, edited by A. Strauss. Chicago: University of Chicago Press.

Piaget, Jean. 1954. The Construction of Reality in the Child. New York: Basic Books.

**Chapter Two**

D'AGNESE, V. PISA's Colonialism: Success, Money, and the Eclipse of Education. Power and Education, [s. l.], v. 7, n. 1, p. 56–72, 2015.

BARTRAM, B. "Career and Money Aside, What's

the Point of University?" A Comparison of Students' Non-Economic Entry Motives in Three European Countries. Higher Education Quarterly, [s. l.], v. 70, n. 3, p. 281–300, 2016.

BROUN, D. Building Capability, Empowering Students, and Achieving Success: The Financial Empowerment for Student Success InitiativeAchieving the Dream. [s. l.]: Achieving the Dream, 2014.

Bowles, Hannah Riley, and Kathleen L. McGinn. 2008. "Gender in Job Negotiations: A Two#Level Game." Negotiation Journal 24, no. 4: 393-410.

Crocker, J., & Wolfe, C. T. (2001). Contingencies of self-worth. Psychological review, 108(3), 593.

Choudhury, M.A. (1997). Money in Islam: A Study in Islamic Political Economy (1st ed.).

FINLEY, A. et al.Is College Worth the Time and Money? It Depends on Whom You AskAssociation of American Colleges and Universities. [s. l.]: Association of American Colleges and Universities,

2021.

Greenacre, P. (1953). Trauma, Growth and Personality (1st ed.). Routledge.

HUNTER, B.; PERRET, R. Can Money Buy Happiness? A Statistical Analysis of Predictors for User Satisfaction. Journal of Academic Librarianship, [s. l.], v. 37, n. 5, p. 402–408, 2011.

HEADEY, B.; MUFFELS, R.; WOODEN, M. Money Does Not Buy Happiness: Or Does It? A Reassessment Based on the Combined Effects of Wealth, Income and Consumption. Social Indicators Research, [s. l.], v. 87, n. 1, p. 65–82, 2008.

Harter, S. (1990). Processes underlying adolescent self-concept formation. In R. Montemayor, G. R. Adams, & T. P. Gullotta (Eds.), From childhood to adolescence: A transitional period? (pp. 205–239). Sage Publications, Inc.

Inzlicht, M., & Schmader, T. (Eds.). (2012). Stereotype threat: Theory, process, and application. Oxford University Press.

Kray, L. J., & Thompson, L. (2005). Gender stereotypes and negotiation performance: An examination of theory and research. In B. M. Staw & R. M. Kramer (Eds.), Research in organizational behavior: An annual series of analytical essays and critical reviews, Vol. 26, pp. 103–182). Elsevier Science/JAI Press.

Laurence, A., Maltby, J., & Rutterford, J. (Eds.). (2008). Women and Their Money 1700-1950: Essays on Women and Finance (1st ed.). Routledge.

LU, Serena Changhong,Self-esteem and Women's Performance in Mixed-Gender Negotiation. January 2015. Academy of Management Annual Meeting Proceedings 2015(1):14296-14296.

Lu, C., Paddock, E. L., & Reb, J. (2015). Self-esteem and Women's Performance in Mixed-Gender Negotiation. In Academy of Management Proceedings (Vol. 2015, No. 1, p. 14296). Briarcliff Manor, NY 10510: Academy of Management.

NEAL-JACKSON, A. "Well, What Did You Expect?": Black Women Facing Stereotype Threat in

Collaborative Academic Spaces at a Predominantly White Institution. Journal of College Student Development, [s. l.], v. 61, n. 3, p. 317–332, 2020.

Pyszczynski, T., Greenberg, J., Solomon, S., Arndt, J., & Schimel, J. (2004). Why Do People Need Self-Esteem? A Theoretical and Empirical Review. Psychological Bulletin, 130(3), 435–468.

REED, R. J.; HURD, B. A Value beyond Money? Assessing the Impact of Equity Scholarships: From Access to Success. Studies in Higher Education, [s. l.], v. 41, n. 7, p. 1236–1250, 2016.

SMITH, T. A. Not Just the Raising of Money: Hampton Institute and Relationship Fundraising, 1893-1917. History of Education Quarterly, [s. l.], v. 61, n. 1, p. 63–93, 2021.

SPUHLERA, B. K.; DEW, J. Sound Financial Management and Happiness: Economic Pressure and Relationship Satisfaction as Mediators. Journal of Financial Counseling and Planning, [s. l.], v. 30, n. 2, p. 157–174, 2019.

Stuhlmacher, A. F., & Walters, A. E. (1999). Gender differences in negotiation outcome: A meta-analysis. Personnel Psychology, 52(3), 653-677.

SARRACINO, F. Money, Sociability and Happiness: Are Developed Countries Doomed to Social Erosion and Unhappiness? Time-Series Analysis of Social Capital and Subjective Well-Being in Western Europe, Australia, Canada and Japan. Social Indicators Research, [s. l.], v. 109, n. 2, p. 135–188, 2012.

WOLF, W. C., Jr. The Epistemology of Innovator Motivation. Clearing House, [s. l.], v. 53, n. 2, p. 74–78, 1979.

**Chapter Three**

James, William (1890), The Principles of Psychology.

James, T. (2017). Time Line Therapy and the Basis of Personality: and the basis of personality. Crown House Publishing Ltd.

McLeod, S. (2007). Maslow's hierarchy of needs. Simply psychology, 1(1-18).

# About the Author

Dr Hichem Karoui is a highly respected and accomplished academic, author, and researcher in the field of Sociology. He currently holds a PhD from Sorbonne University (Paris III). He has published an astonishing 49 books on various topics ranging from Middle-East societies and international relations to Muslims in Europe, self-improvement, Happiness and social dynamics. His latest book, "Treatise on Self-improvement," is sure to be a classic. With a curious mind and an eye for detail, Dr Karoui continues to explore the depths of human behaviour and its relation to contemporary society. He shares his knowledge through lectures, seminars, and publications – hoping to help others understand and improve their lives.

Personal Website: https://hichemkaroui.net/


Publisher: Global East-West for Studies and Publishing. London (UK)

www.ingramcontent.com/pod-product-compliance
Lightning Source LLC
Chambersburg PA
CBHW050523160726

48003CB00001B/435